Contents

Language of instruction
   True or false   5
   Questions and answers   6
   Words for comparing   7

Weight and capacity
   Pour and weigh   8
   Weighing   9
   On the shelf   10
   Loading and unloading   11
   Full and empty   12

Manipulating money
   Money matters   13
   Shopping with pocket money   14
   Saving up pocket money   15
   Shopping mall 1   16
   Shopping mall 2   17
   Shopping for tea   18

Manipulating length
   Using yourself to measure   19
   Words for measure   20
   Metric lengths   21
   Measuring in metric lengths   22
   School sizes   23
   American football games   24
   American football gameboard   25

Working with time
   Which day?   26
   Calendar   27
   Changing times 1   28
   Changing times 2   29
   TV and video times   30

Problem solving
   Measure review – picture problems   31
   Measure review – word problems   32

Teachers' notes

Aims of this book

All the practical activities in this book cover main broad issues in Measure. As activity sheets, the photocopiables are designed to encourage independent thinking and working, consolidate skills and raise understanding through discussion. As exemplars, they also provide a valuable resource for teachers and ancillary helpers to build upon.

Using this book

Each themed group of activity sheets has been arranged so as to ensure a natural skill progression appropriate to pupils with special needs. Teachers may wish to use particular sheets or themed groups to consolidate work done in another context. Where it is intended that pupils cut out word lists (prompt cards) from the sheets, these sheets have been designed so that they can still be kept filed as a record of work.

Teacher support

Once the initial instructions on each activity sheet have been explained to the pupil, the activities should be worked through independently. Where further teacher involvement is needed, the sheets give the instruction 'Tell someone'; or the need for extra supervision is pointed out in the teachers' notes.

Mathematical language

Most pupils in our classrooms assimilate mathematical language readily through their regular exposure to basic signs and symbols. However, many pupils with special needs do not find this easy. They need constant prompts to remind them what it all means. This book thus features a set of seven key **prompt cards**. These should be cut out and accumulated to provide the pupil with a personal prompt pack that can be referred to during work on the activity sheets (and at other times). The language on the sheets has been kept to a basic minimum, though you may wish to add to the prompt cards once the idea has been established and individual needs increase. The prompt cards may be used for other reading and writing activities, increasing the extent of the pupils' independent work.

The best way to use the prompt card packs is to access them regularly. Teachers, ancillary helpers, parents and peers can all support pupils' learning and reinforcement of key vocabulary. Before any new activity sheet is attempted, a review of the relevant vocabulary will help the pupils to read and carry out the instructions independently. The prompt cards can be used in three main ways: as a repetitive teaching aid; as a constant visual prompt for the pupils; and as an aid towards independent completion of work.

Notes on individual activities

Page 5: True or false
This activity is designed to introduce pupils to the key instructional vocabulary used in other activity sheets: *read, write, ask, cut* and *stick*. The cutting and sticking skills required here will be used in assembling the prompt card pack; help may be needed to establish a method to be followed in future independent working. The 'true or false' statements given help pupils to think about how much they already know about relative measures in real life. The relevant mathematical skills and concepts will be introduced through practical contexts in the book.

Page 6: Questions and answers
This activity uses question and answer formats to introduce the concept of estimation. Help may be needed initially with recording, but the vocabulary and the picture prompts are intended to encourage independent work. Suitable answers are: people on a bus 30 (single-decker) or 80 (double-decker); length of a pencil 15cm; weight of a feather 1g; weight of a brick 1kg; length of a TV programme probably ½ hour; length of a football match 1½ hours.
Extension activity: Make a 'Sense and Nonsense' game using similar ideas to the ones given. Pupils can write measure questions with multiple-choice answers (including highly unrealistic options) on separate cards, then ask one another for either a Sense answer or a Nonsense answer.

Page 7: Words for comparing
To discuss measure in mathematical language, pupils need to understand and use comparative terms. This activity encourages the pupils to use observation and common knowledge in order to relate comparative and superlative terms to measure. It can be used to consolidate the instruction formats presented on pages 5 and 6; and it also introduces the process of cutting out a word list and sticking it onto card, making a prompt card which can be used later.

Page 8: Pour and weigh
This activity requires the pupil to relate the ideas of pouring and weighing to simple practical examples. It also reinforces the handling of prompt cards. The pupils should read the words on the two cards and discuss any which are unfamiliar. The completed sheet should provide some key discussion points, such as the distinction between *quantity* and *capacity* (use examples to clarify).

Page 9: Weighing
After the general introduction to this subject on page 8, this activity uses practical work to develop the pupils' understanding. They will need access to a balance and some general classroom materials (see activity sheet) in order to carry out the activity; they should experiment with different objects in order to fill in the blanks on the sheet. The 'weigh' prompt card from page 8 may be helpful if the pupils are not familiar with metric units of weight.
Extension activity: Pupils could start to collect food labels with the weight printed on, to improvise games of Swap or Snap with weight as the focus.

Page 10: On the shelf
This activity presents addition and subtraction in the context of comparing and making up weights. Implicitly, a distinction is made between weight and size. The 'weigh' prompt card may be helpful.
Extension activity: The pupils could collect food labels and try to make up a basket of a given weight, or balance their shopping equally between two bags.

Page 11: Loading and unloading
This sheet involves multiplication (or repeated addition) of larger weights. This requires a proficiency in using 2× tables and in counting in 5s and 10s. The final drawing task assesses the pupils' grasp of the appropriate visual imagery.
Extension activity: Pupils could be set problems involving the combination of different weights to reach a maximum total weight – for example, an aircraft hold requiring an equal distribution of weight between two compartments.

Page 12: Full and empty
The practical activities on this sheet will require some supervision and explanation. The only units involved here are quarters of a bottle. If they follow the instructions correctly, the pupils should obtain full, half-full, one-quarter-full and three-quarters-full bottles, and be able to label them. The 'Pour' prompt card from page 8 may be helpful as a starting point. Further the discussion by using marked bottles (1 litre or 1 pint) and asking the pupils to give answers as fractions of this capacity unit.
Extension activity: The pupils could try making sounds by tapping the mouths of glass bottles filled to different extents with water ('capacity music').

Page 13: Money matters
Most pupils with special educational needs at Key Stage 2 have a working knowledge of money and coins, but may require further experience of manipulating, changing, saving and spending money. This activity and the five that follow provide suitable opportunities for pupils to extend their understanding. The teacher may wish to check their coin recognition using real (or plastic) money, which should be available as a resource for these activities. The filling of purses to hold £1 in various coin values may be extended by using a mixture of values.
Extension activity: The game described in Figure 1 develops pupils' ability to manipulate coins to £1.

> **Money Man**
> Make the Money Man with a dice. First put a sticker for each amount (50p, 20p, 10p, 5p, 2p, 1p) on each face. Then throw the dice and match the throw to a body part. Draw the parts of the Money Man. The winner is the first player to make a complete drawing.
>
> *Figure 1*

Page 14: Shopping with pocket money

The prompt card on this sheet introduces the shopping vocabulary used in the next four activities. Pupils may need some initial help to read the words, but the card will increase their ability to work independently on the tasks. This activity extends the recognition and manipulation of coins from £1 to £2.50, and allows an element of choice.

Extension activity: A variety of shopping trips can be devised. Collecting data on what items are bought by the pupils can produce lively discussion, or be represented in a graph for interpretation.

Page 15: Saving up pocket money

This activity requires either repeated addition or use of the 4× table. It also introduces the idea of change (from £10) in the context of creative shopping. The mental images of coin values built up in the two previous activities should help the pupils to perform relatively complex mental arithmetic tasks.

Extension activity: The creative shopping box could be used several times, concentrating on themed buying: food items, clothes, magazines.

Pages 16 and 17: Shopping Mall 1 and 2

This double-sheet activity involves shopping with the more realistic sum of £100. The pictorial shops may need to be visited in discussion before the written activities can be done independently. The prompt card on page 14 may be helpful for some pupils. The work on both sheets consolidates skills already covered (comparison, sorting, adding up a bill and calculating change), as well as requiring some personal creative thinking. Page 17 may need to be worked through a few times.

Extension activity: A parent may limit spending in various ways, such as saying 'No more than £50 on clothes!' How would this affect the pupils' choices? Alternatively, the pupils could design their own Shopping Mall and shopping game.

Page 18: Shopping for tea

This activity develops the idea of adding up a bill and calculating change. Calculators could be provided for less confident pupils. The activity can be completed independently if the picture prompts are interpreted correctly. In the first instance a set shopping list is provided. All costing is in round figures for ease of calculation. The prompt card from page 14 may be helpful. (This activity should be attempted before the double-page 'Shopping Mall' activity.)

Extension activity: See bottom of sheet. The pupils could also design their own supermarket, selling their favourite foods at realistic prices.

Page 19: Using yourself to measure

The teacher will need to be involved in this activity, both physically and as instructor. The activity revisits estimation (see page 6) by using spans, cubits and paces as units of length. The practical task is followed by reasoning and discussion in appropriate mathematical language. The pupil should conclude that the size of a span or a cubit depends on the person using the measurement. Ideally, after initial instruction, the pupils should work independently with the co-operation of friends and the teacher, gathering information for subsequent analysis. This activity helps the pupil to appreciate the difference between standard and non-standard measures.

Page 20: Words for measure

The prompt card introduces specific terms related to the measurement of length or distance; the teacher may need to explain these words and how they are related. The instructions may need to be talked through before the pupils complete the activity. Practical examples of objects, with the dimensions being pointed out, may also be helpful.

Extension activity: The pupils could be asked to estimate and then measure distances in paces, such as the distance from home to the bus stop.

Page 21: Metric lengths

This activity introduces a 20cm ruler length as a practical basis for work on metric measurement. It repeats the work in the 'Using yourself to measure' activity in the context of metric units. The 20cm strip could be made up to 1m for use in the next two activities, and could be made durable in various ways (stuck onto card, laminated and so on). On completion, a discussion will help the pupils to accomplish other measuring tasks.

Page 22: Measuring in metric lengths

The activity consolidates and extends the previous measuring work, revisiting the concepts of length, width and height while requiring the pupils to convert centimetres to metres. Some discussion of three-dimensional objects in terms of words like 'thickness', 'depth' and 'width' may be necessary.

Extension activity: Pupils could make a 1m height tape (by sticking together five 20cm tapes from the previous activity) to measure the heights of the class members. The data can be displayed as a bar chart.

Page 23: School sizes

This activity consolidates the use of comparative language and conversion from cm to m. It requires the pupils to judge distances using a pictorial representation with a scale. The pupils may need some discussion time to complete the activity successfully and with understanding. The prompt card from page 20 may be helpful. Measuring the heights of classmates and adults (using a height tape fixed to a wall or door), with similar questions being posed, will help to consolidate this experience.

Extension activity: School plans can provide useful starting points for discussion of the design of school buildings: dimensions, building materials and so on.

Pages 24 and 25: American football game

This activity provides reinforcement of previous learning. Page 24 can be cut into three cards: an introductory card and two game cards. Some supervision may be required to get Game 1 underway, but play should then continue unaided. Game 2 is more demanding than Game 1: it requires the child to place the ball more accurately (in 5m zones), and to add up the cumulative score exactly (using the scorecards on page 25) rather than counting in tens. The pupils should play Game 1 several times before attempting Game 2.

Extension activity: The pupils could set up league tables or play a challenge cup.

Page 26: Which day?

The prompt card on this sheet introduces the vocabulary on which all the activities in this section are based. Some initial instruction with this vocabulary will benefit the pupils' future independent work, as will some brief discussion on the completion of each activity. The word 'birthday' appears on the prompt card but not in the activities, since some pupils may be unsure of their birthdays; you may wish to suggest finding birthdays on a calendar. This sheet and the next introduce time measure in broad terms; they will be helpful for pupils who have difficulty with sequencing, as they reinforce basic time sequences: relating the days of the week to the concepts of 'today', 'yesterday' and 'tomorrow'.

Extension activity: The names of days could be written on cards and used for sorting and matching.

Page 27: Calendar

This activity consolidates the pupils' knowledge of the days of the week and the months of the year, as well as introducing the calendar structure for the arrangement of days. The leap year arrangement could be discussed. The activity could be reinforced by the 'Rain or Shine' game shown in Figure 2, where the rules provide an element of choice and mathematical problem-solving.

Extension activity: The pupils could arrange a set of 'months of the year' cards in order, perhaps grouping them according to season.

Page 28 and 29: Changing times 1 and 2

These activities lead pupils to explore how the time of day can be represented in analog and digital formats. The words on the prompt card and the text in the activity should be clearly understood before the clock activities are attempted. The examples shown on the clocks pinpoint basic time manipulation skills in translating from analog to digital and vice versa. Further examples could be devised for more complete practice in these skills; only quarter-hour divisions are shown here. The concept of the 24-hour clock may require more consolidation.

Page 30: TV and video times

This activity uses the pupils' probable familiarity with the representation of programme times on television. The pupils may also be familiar with the use of a digital clock to set a video recorder; however, they do not need this experience to make sense of the activity. Some help may be needed with the recording of times in analog and digital format. The prompt card from page 28 may also be helpful.

Extension activity: Data on favourite programmes could be collected within groups or the class, and be presented in various ways. The time measurement aspect of this data should be emphasised.

Page 31: Measure review – picture problems

These revision problems use picture prompts to show relationships between measured quantities. One example in each category of measure (weight, capacity, quantity, length and time) is given. Many more suitable examples can be found in maths puzzle books. Pupils may find the prompt card pack built up from previous activity sheets helpful.

Page 32: Measure review – word problems

In these revision problems, the picture prompt has been reduced to a minimum; the challenge is to interpret the written information in order to work out a successful answer. The examples constitute a fair overall review of the skills gained. Pupils may find the prompt card pack helpful. In problem 2, the pupils should notice that 8:30am and 8:30pm look the same on an analog clock (but not a digital clock).

These two review sheets could be used to make an initial assessment of pupils' ability in measure, so that appropriate support activities can be chosen from these resources. They are also useful as 'busy sheets' for other pupils.

Rain or Shine – a calendar game

You will need: 2 players, a page from an old calendar, counters, 2 dice.
One player is 'rain' with dark counters.
One player is 'shine' with light counters.
Take turns to throw the 2 dice. You can use the numbers thrown in either of these ways:
- Add them, for example 1 + 3 = 4.
- Combine them, for example 1 and 3 makes 13 or 31.

Each player can decide, make a date and put a counter on it.
When all the days are covered in dark or light counters, see who has won: 'Rain' or 'Shine'.

Figure 2

◆ ESSENTIALS FOR MATHS: Understanding measures

◆ Name _____

True or false

Before you could read or write you learned many things about Measure.

You will need: a pen or a pencil, scissors, glue, blank card.

◆ Think about these.
Are they true? Write True or False.

An elephant is bigger than a mouse. _____

A mother is bigger than a baby. _____

A sweet is heavier than a brick. _____

Cars go faster than bicycles. _____

You can drink a bucket of milk. _____

◆ Make up some more. Make some true and some false.
For example:

A lion is bigger than an ant.	True
A thin man weighs more than a fat man.	False

◆ To make a quiz game, cut these out and stick them on to blank card.
Make up a True or False game. The player with the most True cards wins!
You may need more questions to make your game more interesting.

◆ Name _____

Questions and answers

To *estimate*, we make a sensible guess.
◆ Read the question... then choose a sensible guess from the answers.

You will need: a pen or a pencil.

Q How many people can fill a bus?

A _____   2   30   80   200

Q How long is a pencil?

A _____   2cm   15cm   1 metre

Q How light is a feather?

A _____   5g   1g   100g

Q How heavy is a brick?

A _____   10kg   1kg   100g

Q How long is:

your favourite TV programme?

a football match?

3 hours   5 minutes   ½ hour   5 hours   1½ hours   10 minutes

◆ Write your answers here.

My favourite TV programme is _____ long.

A football match is _____ long.

◆ Can you estimate how many full cups you can pour from a pint of milk?

_____ Try to check your answer!

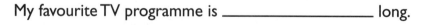

◆ ESSENTIALS FOR MATHS: Understanding measures   6

◆ Name _____

Words for comparing

To compare things, you need the words on the prompt card at the bottom of this page.
◆ Read them to someone.

◆ Look at this:

|— long —|

|— longer —|

|— longest —|

◆ Draw pictures to show:

| |
| |
| tall   taller   tallest |

| |
| |
| small   smaller   smallest |

◆ Complete these:

An elephant is bigger than _____ .

_____ is wider than a river.

A brick is heavier than _____ .

◆ Answer these questions:

Who is the tallest in the class?

_____

Who has the shortest hair?

_____

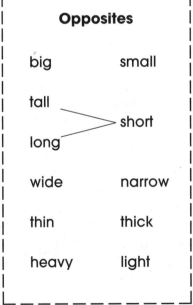

You will need: a pen or a pencil, scissors, glue, blank card.

Opposites

big — small

tall ⎫
    ⎬— short
long ⎭

wide — narrow

thin — thick

heavy — light

◆ Cut out and stick this prompt card as your teacher shows you. Keep it to use again.

ESSENTIALS FOR MATHS: Understanding measures

◆ Name _____

Pour and weigh

◆ Look at the picture, then put the words in the right box.
Read the words on the two prompt cards at the bottom of the page.

You will need:
a pen or pencil, scissors, glue, blank card.

You pour these things:

You weigh these things:

◆ Fill in the missing word:

I would weigh _____ (myself, apples, pop) on the kitchen scales.

I would weigh _____ (potatoes, myself, sugar) on the bathroom scales.

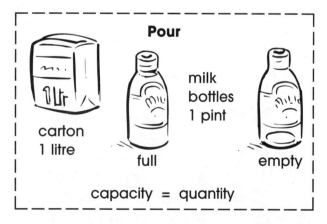

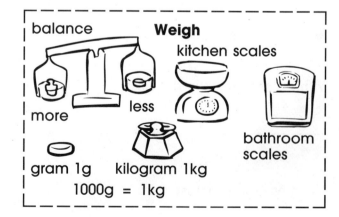

◆ Cut out and stick these two prompt cards.

◆ ESSENTIALS FOR MATHS: Understanding measures

◆ Name _____

Weighing

You will need: a balance, a pen or a pencil.

This balance works like a see-saw. It is used to weigh things by balancing them with one another.

◆ Find these things:

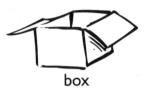   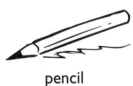

box   book   ball   pencil   Plasticine   blocks

◆ Weigh them in the balance and complete this list:

Object		Object
_____	is heavier than	_____
_____	is heavier than	_____
_____	is lighter than	_____
_____	is lighter than	_____
_____	is the same as	_____

◆ Using the 'Weigh' prompt card to help you, work out how many grams these weights are:

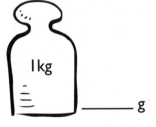 ____ g   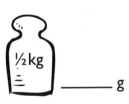 ____ g   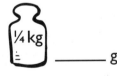 ____ g   gram ____ g

The weights could be used on the scales in a shop.
◆ List some things that might be weighed in a shop.

_____ _____ _____ _____

_____ _____ _____ _____

◆ ESSENTIALS FOR MATHS: Understanding measures

◆ Name _____

On the shelf

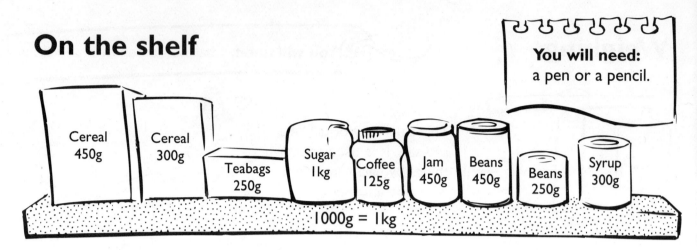

You will need:
a pen or a pencil.

1000g = 1kg

◆ Look at the goods on the shelf. Write them next to the correct weights:

Weight 450g _____ _____ _____

Weight 300g _____ _____ _____

Weight 250g _____ _____ _____

Weight 125g _____

_____ weighs more than _____.

_____ weighs less than _____.

_____ weighs the same as _____.

◆ Draw the goods needed to balance a 1kg bag of sugar.

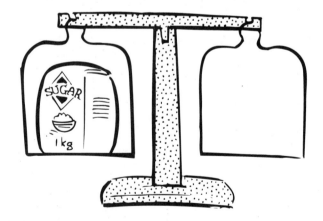   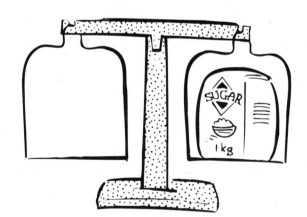

◆ Complete this:
1kg sugar weighs the same as

_____ plus _____ plus _____.

ESSENTIALS FOR MATHS: Understanding measures

◆ Name _____

Loading and unloading

This empty lorry can carry 100kg. These packs are 10kg each.

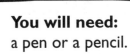

You will need:
a pen or a pencil.

Loading

◆ How many packs can the lorry carry? _____

A forklift truck is used to carry 2 packs each time.

How many trips will be needed to load the lorry? _____

How many kg will the forklift carry each trip? _____

Unloading

This full lorry holds 500kg. Each pack to unload weighs 50kg.
The forklift can only carry one of these packs at a time.

◆ How many trips will it make to unload the lorry? _____

◆ Draw a lorry full with 50kg packs. It can carry 200kg.

ESSENTIALS FOR MATHS: Understanding measures

◆ Name _____

Full and empty

You will need: 3 empty plastic bottles (all the same size), a funnel, a sink with a tap, a pen or a pencil.

◆ Do this at a sink:

1. Fill one bottle to the top with water. This full bottle is one measure.
2. Pour equal amounts of water from the full bottle into the two empty ones, using a funnel.
3. Draw the result below.

How much is in bottle 2 and bottle 3?
_____ _____

4. Leave bottle 3. Take the empty bottle 1. Make it and bottle 2 look the same by pouring water from bottle 2 into bottle 1.
Draw the result on the right.

How much is in each bottle?
_____

5. Pour *one* of these amounts into bottle 3.
Draw how much water is in bottle 3 now.

You have poured from: | full | to | ½ full | to | ¼ full | to | ¾ full |

◆ Write the amounts under these bottles:

full _____ _____ _____ _____ empty

Bottles can measure different amounts, such as a pint or a litre, depending on their size. What size did you use? Tell someone.

◆ Name _____

Money matters

You will need: a pencil, coins to help you.

◆ Draw enough coins in each purse to make £1.

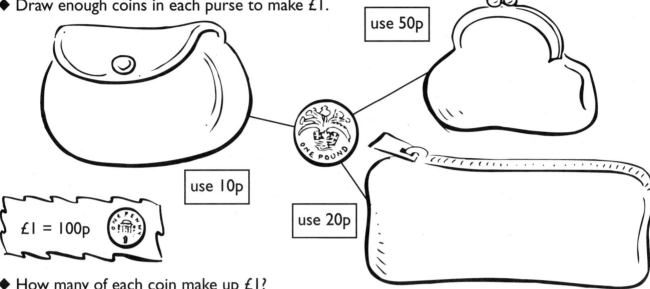

use 50p

use 10p

use 20p

£1 = 100p

◆ How many of each coin make up £1?

£1	50p	20p	10p	5p	pennies
					100

◆ Make a Money Man.
Use these coins to draw round:

One 50p for body

One 20p for neck

One 10p for head

Two 5ps for hands

Two 1ps for arms

Four 2ps for legs

Money Man

◆ Add up the total.
How much is he worth?

◆ Name _____

Shopping with pocket money

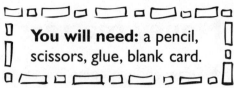
You will need: a pencil, scissors, glue, blank card.

◆ Draw the coins here:

Ann gets £1.50 a week.

Dan gets £2 a week.

Ahmed gets £2.50 a week.

They like to spend some of their pocket money on these things:

magazine 50p   chocolate bar 40p   comic 30p   crisps 20p   swap card 10p   liquorice 5p

Ann spends £1, Dan spends £1.50, Ahmed spends £2.
◆ Write what each one chooses in the right box:

£2	_____ chooses
£1.50	_____ chooses
£1	_____ chooses

◆ Read the shopping words on the prompt card.

```
cash        cost
      buy
total       most
            bill
pay         amount
        price
value       least
      change
```

◆ Cut out and stick this prompt card. Keep it with your other cards.

◆ ESSENTIALS FOR MATHS: Understanding measures   14

◆ Name _____

Saving up pocket money

You will need: a pen or pencil, coins.

Dan, Ann and Ahmed are saving up their pocket money. Here are 4 weeks' savings. Add them up in each money box.

Dan
Pocket money
£2 a week

Ann
Pocket money
£1.50 a week

Ahmed
Pocket money
£2.50 a week

Total savings
£ _____

Total savings
£ _____

Total savings
£ _____

◆ Who has saved the most money? _____

◆ Who has saved the least money? _____

They all want to save £10 for a shopping trip.
◆ How much more does:

Dan need? _____   Ann need? _____   Ahmed need? _____

◆ How soon will they have enough? Today, next week, in a few weeks?

Dan: _____   Ann: _____

Ahmed: _____

◆ Draw here what *you* would buy with £10. Write the cost of each thing.

Is there any change left? _____

ESSENTIALS FOR MATHS: Understanding measures

Shopping mall 1

You will need: a pen or a pencil, a calculator.

SHOE HOUSE
Trainers £30
Boots £45

FAB FASHIONS
Jeans £35
T-shirt £15

FOOTBALL WORLD
Football shirt £35
Scarf £15

MUSIC STORE
CDs £10 £15
Videos £10 £15
Computer game £40

SPORT SHELF
Cycle helmet £20
Skateboard £15

JEWELLER'S
Watches
£25 analog
£15 digital

You have £100 to spend.
◆ Look in all the shops before you buy anything.
◆ Complete this list:

_____ costs more than _____

_____ costs more than _____

_____ costs less than _____

_____ costs less than _____

_____ costs the same as _____

Make a list of *all* the items in the shops:

less than £25 each	more than £25 each

ESSENTIALS FOR MATHS: Understanding measures

◆ Name _____

Shopping mall 2

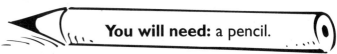
You will need: a pencil.

◆ Draw here the items *you* would choose to buy for £100. Write how much they cost.

Total cost: _____

How much have you spent? _____   How much change is left from £100? _____

◆ List three other ways to spend £100 in the shopping mall:

List 1 £	List 2 £	List 3 £

◆ Look at these lists and *your* choice.   Which list has the fewest things? _____

Which list has the most things? _____   Which list has the best things? _____

◆ Draw any other things you would like to buy from the shopping mall. Write how much they cost, up to a total of £100.

Total cost: _____

ESSENTIALS FOR MATHS: Understanding measures

◆ Name _____

Using yourself to measure

These parts of the body can be used to measure:

You will need: a pen or a pencil, a friend, the teacher.

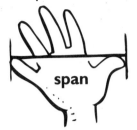

your hand

span = thumb to little finger

your arm

cubit = elbow to tip of fingers

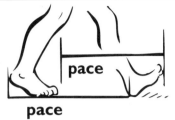

your legs and feet

pace = from heel to heel or from toe to toe

These are **approximate** measures. They can be used to **estimate** distances.
You will learn why this is.

◆ Choose 5 classroom objects, big and small, to estimate the size of.
Use spans and cubits to complete this chart:

objects	yourself	a friend	the teacher
table top	_____ spans _____ cubits	_____ spans _____ cubits	_____ spans _____ cubits
	_____ spans _____ cubits	_____ spans _____ cubits	_____ spans _____ cubits
	_____ spans _____ cubits	_____ spans _____ cubits	_____ spans _____ cubits
	_____ spans _____ cubits	_____ spans _____ cubits	_____ spans _____ cubits
	_____ spans _____ cubits	_____ spans _____ cubits	_____ spans _____ cubits

◆ Take paces across the classroom from wall to wall, then fill in this chart:

pace wall to wall	yourself	a friend	teacher
	_____ paces	_____ paces	_____ paces

◆ Look at the results.
What do you learn about these measures?
Use the words *same*, *bigger*, *smaller* to explain to someone.

◆ Name _____

Words for measure

You will need: a pen or a pencil, scissors, glue, blank card.

To measure accurately, we ask:

How big?
How tall? ⟶ for height
How high?

How long?
How far? ⟶ for length

How wide? ⟶ for width

◆ Read the words on the prompt card at the bottom of the sheet.

◆ What would you use to measure:

• the length of the side of this sheet? _____ ask How big?

• your height? _____ ask _____

• the width of the classroom? _____ ask _____

• the length of your coat? _____ ask _____

• the distance from school to your home? _____ ask _____

Ways we can travel distances:

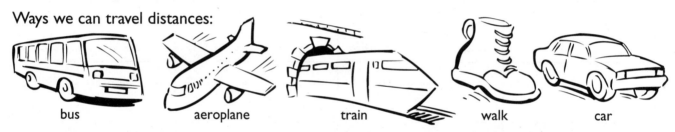

bus   aeroplane   train   walk   car

◆ Choose and draw one of these in the boxes, depending on how far you have to go. Write underneath which way of travelling you have chosen.

Going on holiday

Going to school	Going to town

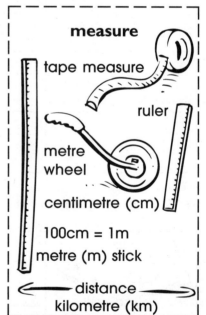

measure

tape measure

ruler

metre wheel

centimetre (cm)

100cm = 1m

metre (m) stick

⟵ distance ⟶
kilometre (km)

◆ Cut out and stick the card. Keep it with your other cards.

◆ ESSENTIALS FOR MATHS: Understanding measures

◆ Name _____

Metric lengths

You will need: a pen or a pencil, scissors, glue.

The ruler opposite is marked in centimetres (cm).

◆ Measure some things with it:

length of your finger _____ cm   length of a pencil _____ cm

length of your hand _____ cm   width of a book _____ cm

These are accurate measures.

◆ Estimate these bigger things in centimetres:

length of your foot _____ cm   width of the table top _____ cm

length of your leg _____ cm   width of a box _____ cm

◆ How could you check your estimates?
◆ Make a centimetre tape to check. You will need to cut out this ruler and the blank one at the bottom of the page.

Mark the centimetres. Go from 21 to _____.
Ask someone to help you to do this.

Stick them together on the shaded parts.

```
| 0                              20 | 21                     |
                                    stick
```

You now have a _____ cm ruler.

◆ Measure with your ruler:

your foot _____ cm

your leg _____ cm

the table top _____ cm

a box _____ cm

Tell someone how accurate your estimates were.

◆ ESSENTIALS FOR MATHS: Understanding measures   21

◆ Name _____

Measuring in metric lengths

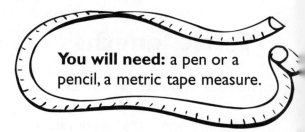

You will need: a pen or a pencil, a metric tape measure.

◆ Look carefully at the marks on the tape measure. You will see centimetres (cm) and metres (m) marked.
100cm = 1m.

◆ Use the metric tape to measure a table top.

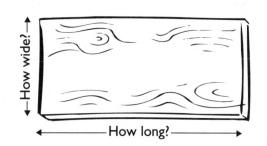

How long? _____ cm

How long? _____ m

How wide? _____ cm

How wide? _____ m

Did you change the centimetres to metres when you got past 100?
◆ Do the same with:

chair

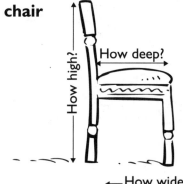

How high? _____ cm

How high? _____ m

How wide? _____ cm

How wide? _____ m

door

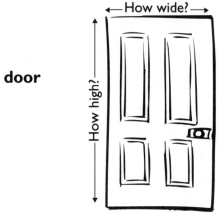

How high?

_____ m _____ cm

How wide?

_____ m _____ cm

cupboard

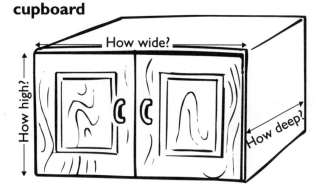

_____ m _____ cm wide

_____ m _____ cm deep

_____ m _____ cm high

◆ ESSENTIALS FOR MATHS: Understanding measures

◆ Name _____

School sizes

You will need: a pen or a pencil.

Here is a school building.
It has two storeys.

How high is the ceiling on the second storey? _____ m

How high is the top of the roof? _____ m

How high is the top of the door? _____ m

◆ Draw a window for the second storey.

Estimate how long it is: _____ m

Estimate how wide it is: _____ m

◆ Look at the class by the door.
Estimate the following heights:

the teacher _____ cm = _____ m _____ cm

the helper _____ cm = _____ m _____ cm

Dan _____ cm = _____ m _____ cm

Ann _____ cm = _____ m _____ cm

Ahmed _____ cm = _____ m _____ cm

Zack _____ cm = _____ m _____ cm

Zoë _____ cm = _____ m _____ cm

Who is the tallest in the class? _____

at _____ m _____ cm

Who is the shortest? _____

at _____ m _____ cm

How many people in the class are taller than I metre? _____

teacher   helper   Dan   Ann   Ahmed   Zack   Zoë

◆ ESSENTIALS FOR MATHS: Understanding measures

◆ Name _____

American football games

Choose a team:

Miami Dolphins    Dallas Cowboys

Chicago Bears   Washington

NY Giants    Redskins

You will need: 3 dice, 2 counters, the game board.

Use the game board opposite.
One player plays from each end, starting at the 0m line.
Your aim is to score by reaching the other **Endzone**.

Game 1 – 2 players

Both players put a counter (for a ball) on their START line.
The first player throws 3 dice. Add the scores:

_____ + _____ + _____ = _____.

If you score more than 10, move to 10m line. Take another turn.
If you score more than 10 again, keep moving to the next metre line and so on.
If you score less than 10, the second player gets to throw the dice and move.
When you reach the **Endzone** you score a goal!
Return to the START line to start again.

The **winner** is the first player to score 5 goals.

Game 2 – 2 players

In this game the pitch is marked in 5m zones for accuracy in scoring.
Both players put a counter in their 0–5m zone.
The players take turns to throw 3 dice and add the scores, placing the counter in the right zone and keeping an accurate score on the score card.
Keep adding to your score, up to 100. Move your counter into the right zone for your cumulative (added up) score each time,
e.g. 5+, 10+, 15+, 20+ and so on.
A score of 100+ reaches the **Endzone** and scores a goal.

The **winner** is the first player to score 3 goals, or the player with the highest score on the scorecard.

◆ ESSENTIALS FOR MATHS: Understanding measures

◆ Name _____

American football gameboard

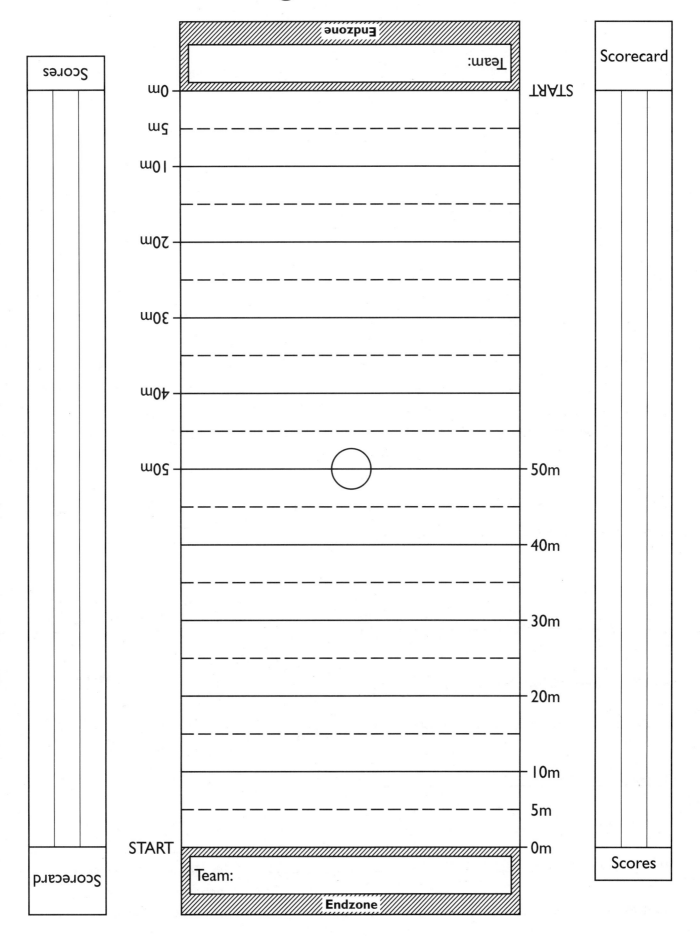

◆ ESSENTIALS FOR MATHS: Understanding measures   25

◆ Name _____

Which day?

You will need: a pen or a pencil, scissors, glue, blank card.

◆ There are seven days in one week.
Write the name of each day, starting with Monday.
Use the diagram on the right to help you.

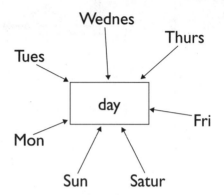

1st day = _____

2nd day = _____

3rd day = _____

4th day = _____

5th day = _____

6th day = _____

7th day = _____

◆ Abbreviations are shorter ways of writing words.
Write the five school days as abbreviations. One has been done for you.

_____ _____ Wed. _____ _____

The weekend days are Sat. and _____.

Write the day before and the day after the weekend.

_____ Sat. Sun. _____

◆ Read the words on the prompt card opposite.

◆ Write dates to complete these sentences.

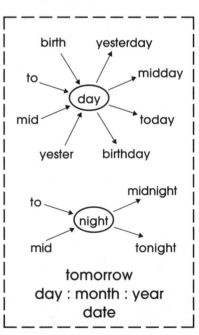

Today is _____

Yesterday was _____

Tomorrow will be _____

Today's date is _____

◆ Cut out and stick this prompt card. Keep it with your other cards.

◆ ESSENTIALS FOR MATHS: Understanding measures   26

◆ Name _____

Calendar

◆ There are 12 months in one year. Here is a poem about them:

You will need: a pen or a pencil.

30 days has September, April, June and November,
All the rest have 31, except February alone,
Which has 28 days clear, and 29 in each leap year.

◆ Copy the months and their abbreviations in the list below. Write the number of days in each month from the saying above. One has been done for you.

1	January	_____	Jan. _____	_____ days
2	February	_____	Feb. _____	_____ days
3	March	_____	Mar. _____	_____ days
4	April	_____	Apr. _____	_____ days
5	May	_____	May _____	_____ days
6	June	_____	June _____	_____ days
7	July	_____	July _____	_____ days
8	August	_____	Aug. _____	_____ days
9	September	_____	Sept. _____	____30____ days
10	October	_____	Oct. _____	_____ days
11	November	_____	Nov. _____	_____ days
12	December	_____	Dec. _____	_____ days

This month is _____					
Sunday					
Monday					
Tuesday					
Wednesday					
Thursday					
Friday					
Saturday					

◆ A calendar shows the days in each month on a page. Fill in this page, naming the month at the top.

You will need to find out:
◆ which was the first day;
◆ how many days this month has.

Write today's date:

_____

◆ ESSENTIALS FOR MATHS: Understanding measures

◆ Name _____

Changing times 1

Clocks and watches tell the time.
They may show it in two different ways.
◆ Read the prompt card at the bottom of the page.

You will need: a pen or pencil, scissors, glue, blank card.

Analog time is shown on a dial as 1–12 hours. There are 12 hours for the night and morning, then another 12 hours for the afternoon and evening.

Digital time is shown as numbers: 0–24 hours for a whole day.
A video recorder shows digital time.
◆ What else shows digital time?

◆ What time is it? Fill in the gaps:

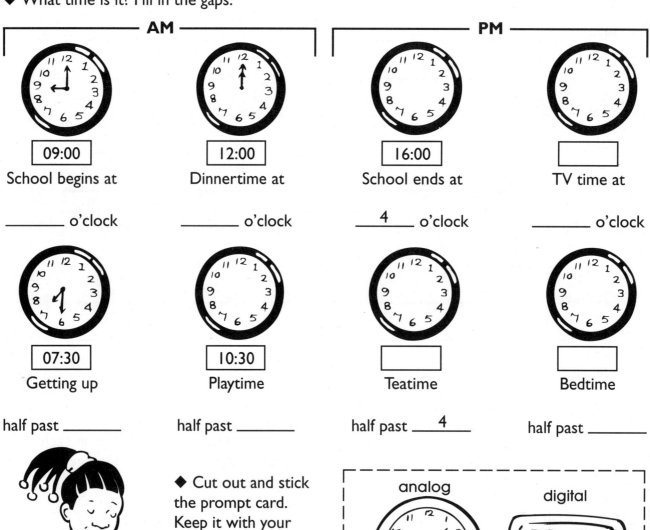

— AM —

09:00	12:00
School begins at	Dinnertime at
_____ o'clock	_____ o'clock

— PM —

16:00	
School ends at	TV time at
__4__ o'clock	_____ o'clock

07:30	10:30		
Getting up	Playtime	Teatime	Bedtime
half past _____	half past _____	half past __4__	half past _____

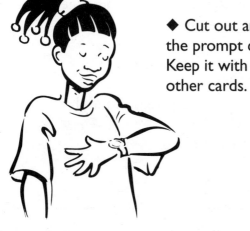

◆ Cut out and stick the prompt card. Keep it with your other cards.

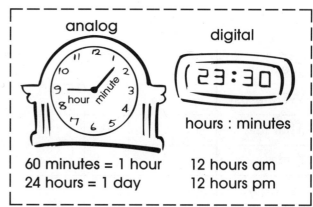

analog — digital
23:30
hours : minutes

60 minutes = 1 hour   12 hours am
24 hours = 1 day   12 hours pm

ESSENTIALS FOR MATHS: Understanding measures

◆ Name _____

Changing times 2

{ You will need: a pen or a pencil. }

◆ Change these times from digital to analog:

| 08:00 | 11:30 | 15:00 | 20:30 | 00:00 |

Please draw a clock face with the numbers on but no hands as shown on the attached sheet. You only need to draw one as we will duplicate it for these other four.

_____ _____ _____ _____ _____

◆ Write the time in words underneath each clock.

◆ Match these times by drawing arrows:

analog	digital
4.00pm	22:00
6.30pm	13:30
10.00pm	15:00
7.00pm	21:30
1.30pm	18:30
3.00pm	16:00
9.30pm	19:00

(arrow drawn from 4.00pm to 22:00)

◆ What time will it be in half an hour?

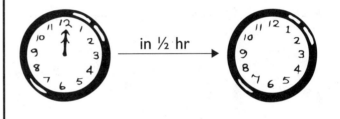

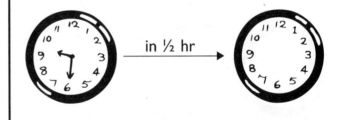

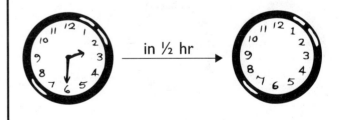

| 22:30 | in ½ hr → | : |

| 00:30 | in ½ hr → | : |

ESSENTIALS FOR MATHS: Understanding measures

◆ Name _____

TV and video times

You will need: a pen or a pencil.

Darren watches TV on Saturday morning and videos the programmes on Tuesday afternoon.

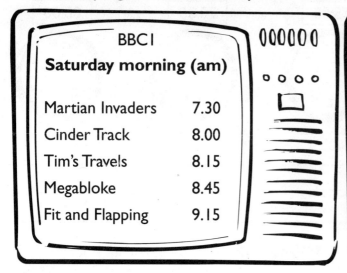

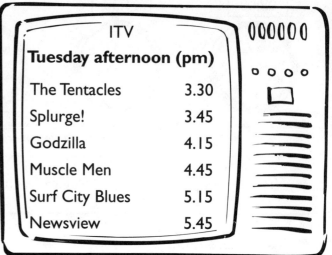

◆ Show analog times for these programmes:

◆ Show the video times (digital, 24-hour):

How long? _____

3.30	3.45
:	:

_____

3.45	4.15
:	:

_____

4.15	4.45
:	:

4.45	5.15
:	:

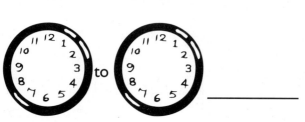

_____

5.15	5.45
:	:

To set the video to record all of these programmes, use the

start time [:]

finish time [:]

Add up the total watching time: _____

How much time is used up on the videotape? _____

◆ ESSENTIALS FOR MATHS: Understanding measures

◆ Name _____

Measure review – picture problems

You will need: a pen or a pencil.

◆ **Calculating weight**

Variety pack

8-pack variety weighs _____ g

Large oat flakes packet weighs _____ g

Weight difference = _____ g

Which would *you* buy? _____

Tell someone why.

◆ **Calculating capacity**

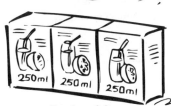

Pack of 3

Big carton of fruit juice contains _____

Small carton contains _____

Pack of 3 small cartons contains _____

Which contains more, one big carton or a pack of

3 small cartons? _____

Which would *you* buy? _____

Tell someone why.

◆ **Calculating quantity**

Half a dozen eggs

6 eggs in a box is _____ dozen.

How many eggs make 1 dozen? _____

How many boxes make 2 dozen eggs? _____

◆ **Calculating length**

Each fence panel is 100cm long.

How many fence panels would you need to go

round this garden? _____

◆ **Calculating time**

How long is a 180-minute blank videotape in hours? _____

How long is a 240-minute blank videotape in hours? _____

How many half-hour programmes can you record on each one?

_____ _____

◆ ESSENTIALS FOR MATHS: Understanding measures

◆ Name _____

Measure review – word problems

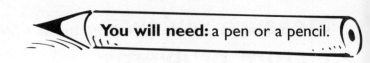 You will need: a pen or a pencil.

1. A money challenge

You have £1. How many cans can you buy? _____

How much for a six-pack? _____   How many six-packs for £3? _____

2. A time challenge

  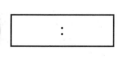

Show half past 8 in the morning and in the evening:

What do you notice about the two analog time clocks? _____

3. Measuring

1 metre = _____ centimetres

What is half a metre? _____ cm   a quarter of a metre? _____ cm

Measure this line:  _____ cm

4. Weighing

How many kg can be weighed on this scale? _____

What other measure marks can you see? _____

What things might be weighed on this scale? _____

5. Capacity

To fill a bucket, you could use a 2-litre jug for pouring. You fill the jug 10 times and pour the water into the bucket. The bucket is now full.

How much is in the bucket? _____

You fill the jug 50 times. How many full buckets? _____

6. Distance

A46	
Lincoln	25km
Newark	50km
Nottingham	75km
Leicester	100km

Which place is furthest away? _____

Which place will you reach first? _____

How far is it on the A46 from:

Lincoln to Newark? _____   Lincoln to Leicester? _____

Which distances are the same? Tell someone.

◆ ESSENTIALS FOR MATHS: Understanding measures